T0124206

The Healing Agenda

NOOR SOI RAMA

authorHOUSE®

AuthorHouse™
1663 Liberty Drive
Bloomington, IN 47403
www.authorhouse.com
Phone: 1 (800) 839-8640

Published by AuthorHouse 05/24/2016

ISBN: 978-1-5246-0540-7 (sc)
ISBN: 978-1-5246-0539-1 (e)

CONTENTS

DEDICATION

To Spirit, the breath of life that resides in us all.

A C K N O W L E D G E M E N T

Thank you Judy Arkwright for your patience as we sat side by side editing the words that seemed to take their own life form as we pondered, What Would Mitch Do?

OVERVIEW

This story is about my personal process with soul healing and the connection with Energy Medicine and Alternative Methods. I am a young woman that is seeking transformation at my very root, to reach the fullest potential in the evolutionary process of life. The outcomes of these stories present encouragement, strength and inspiration that is raw, emotional and real.

In this book, I paint a picture of a young girl growing up without a father figure. The one father figure I had, my grandfather, died when I was seven. My mother worked in a mental institution for 25 years and ended up with two closed head injuries. I couldn't stand living at home with my sick mother anymore, it became to mentally and emotionally taxing. I started working in strip clubs selling my body and soul, looking for fatherly affection; which in turn created deeper issues with lust and money. This only isolated me further away from the love I was seeking.

I invite you as the reader into the shadow side of my own personal life, allowing you into the secret essence of my soul from adult entertainment clubs to the Himalayas. <u>The Healing Agenda</u> allows the reader to learn behind the scenes of my complete full circle journey. A fatherless girl grows up seeking and searching for her own truth and love from the masculine world.

This story is pure, passionate and true. It's the authentic agenda of my personal and spiritual healing from bodywork, natural therapies, hope and faith.

ABOUT THE AUTHOR

Noor was the name given to me by one of my spiritual mentors when I was twenty years young. Noor means The Light. My travels to Peru, lead me to the Shipibo tribe in Pucallpa. They gave me the name Soi Rama, meaning Presence Now.

Noor Soi Rama is the Founder and Spiritual Director of **This Sacred Space, Ahimsa Yoga Wellness Center** and **Energy Medicine Foundations, LLC** in Wyandotte, Michigan. She is a Licensed Massage Therapist, Yoga Instructor, Raw Food Chef, Reiki Master Teacher and a Polarity Therapist. She believes in whole body healing and is the author of several health articles in the *Body, Mind, Spirit Guide and Natural Awakenings Health Guide.*

She has over 10 years experience and certifications in United States, China, India, and Thailand. She worked as a Massage and Yoga

Specialist at the prestigious Amanyara on Turks and Caicos Island, British West Indies. Her daily treatments include: Yoga, Massage, Craniosacral Therapy, Specialized Diets, Detoxes and Energy Medicine. Noor has studied at the National Olympic Training Center in Beijing, China and is certified in Qigong and Tuina.

She lived in India studying at Sivananda Kutir, Himalayas, and with, Surinder Singh in Rishikesh for certification in Yoga and Meditation. Taught and certified by Alissa Cohen herself, Noor became a Raw Food Chef. She attended the Thai Massage School of Chiang Mai, Chiang Mai, Thailand with a certification in Thai Massage. Noor is journeying to become a Traditional Medicine Woman in the Amazonian Rainforest of Peru with indigenous healers.

Noor may be contacted at:
Awakenwithin@hotmail.com
www.thissacredspace.net

Chapter 1

Grandpa's Lap

I can remember being as young as five, sitting at the table with my Grandfather. Surrounded by a table full of pop and junk food consisting of: Faygo pop, cake, candy, cookies, chips, and more chips. He was a large man, diagnosed with diabetes. He took to his sweets, the way that the obesity took to his body. Shoot, thirty years ago the microwave was the main thing at their house. Microwaving boxes of sausage and TV dinners were the norm at Grammy and Grandpa's.

He was hard of hearing, which I came to believe to be optional of Grammy's voice. I can still hear my grandpa, "Hey, hey, I can't hear you," "Dam it, Joe, I know you hear me." He had perfect pitch on his saxophones, which he played in the local town street fair every year. He would take me to the trunk of his Cadillac and play that horn right in my face while I was sipping on Red, Orange, or Rock and Rye Faygo.

He taught me to read sitting on his lap at the kitchen table. Grandpa was the only father figure in my life. He died of a heart attack in his sleep when I was seven. I clearly remember my mom pulling me out of first grade and taking me to the bathroom, to tell me Grandpa had died in his sleep. I inherited his saxophones and took lessons to learn to play. To this day, I feel the essence of his spirit every time I pick up his horns. His words still linger in my mind all these years later, "Good Night, honey."

CHAPTER 2

Mental Striptease

My mother was a single parent. She worked in a mental institution and babysat once she got home to make ends meet. Grammy always watched me. She pretty much raised me, while mom was working. Mom always said my father wasn't interested in kids. That implanted this feeling of sadness, why wouldn't any father want to see and spend time with his children? All my friends' families had dads who were active in their lives, just not mine it seemed. Mom always did what she could and gave me whatever I wanted.

There remained a void. Once I began growing up into my teen years, looking for fatherly love began to run my life. I lustfully gave my body and soul to any man who would have me, thinking that was love. I had no self-worth, no self-love, no sense of self, period. Ava, was my stage name, she easily made $1,000-$2,000 a shift at the club. Interestingly, how money can quickly veil ones false sense of self. It makes my skin fucking crawl to think of how I put my body out there to be used and abused in an effort to fill the fatherly void.

This next story gets told in our circuit of friends over and over. I was three hours away at a Reggae Fest somewhere in Michigan, with some serious party people. We were popping pills of Ecstasy, eating bags of mushrooms, consuming basically anything that was floating around, and then the phone call came.

My mother was on the line, she could barely speak as she told me that she had hit her head and was in the hospital.

What impeccable timing, I was purposefully harming my brain while my mother had accidentally harmed hers. My friend Steve and

I sat in my car smoking a bowl, I needed to get home. He thought that was impossible, of course, given our condition. There was no other option though. My mom had a closed head injury and I needed to get to her. By the grace of God, I somehow made it home within hours to get to the hospital and by her side. The power of one's mind is an incredible thing. Mind over Matter is true. We can always do what we need to do when we need to do it.

I was 19 years young when my mom suffered her first closed head injury. It seemed she had passed out from the blood pressure medication she was taking. The brain is a very tricky organ, especially after it has had severe damage done upon it. Mom came home and slept for weeks, which seemed like forever. She doesn't remember anything. The episodes of screaming and the crying, the moods from a closed head injury are like nothing I have ever experienced before. It is very hard to live with a person suffering from an injury like this. One second they remember something to tell you and the next they are screaming at you and don't even remember what or why.

After about six months of her healing process, she looked and felt better than ever and went back to work at the mental institution. This didn't last long. One of the patients she had accompanied into the elevator, unexpected and viciously punched her in the head. Her brain, bleeding and traumatized for a second time, she was rushed to the hospital.

"Ava you have a phone call. Your mother has been hurt."

"Ava, you are up in two…".

CHAPTER 3

Irene

She was a master, a guru, a natural born healer who could read you better than you could see your own reflection in the mirror.

It was the summer before I turned 21 years young. I'll never forget the clean, fresh scent of walking into the Massage School. Entering the building was like an awakening to all of your senses for the first time. The smiling faces, classrooms filled with eager students, the soft and tranquil music, the love . . . . and Irene.

She had eyes that could see straight to your soul and identify whatever you had hidden in your subconscious mind. She was a short Finnish woman in her early eighties and had been teaching massage and bodywork for over fifty years. She was a true healer. A spark lit inside my soul that day as I locked eyes with her, a deep grounding into the rest of my life. I signed up for classes that day and was admitted into Irene's class. A switch had been flicked on in my being.

Long after the year long course and completion of the program, Irene and I would set up time for me to go to her house and learn more with her. She taught me her insights of energy balancing. She learned her craft from her father who was a natural healer and her good friend John Bodary, who would become my teacher years down the road. She also taught me the entire process of Craniosacral Therapy, which she learned from her longtime friend and colleague, John Upledger.

The Esoteric Healing experiences that happened in her basement changed the course of my existence and opened the doorway to a life of infinite possibilities. She taught me how to develop and trust my intuitive abilities for facilitating the healing process of others. She described that we were merely being a jumper cable for the people to connect with their own source of healing.

My confidence to entrust this intuitiveness entered a new dimension. I witnessed her teachings in action as she worked on my body. I could sense her words on my body and feel them in my mind. I didn't understand at first, but I learned to sense how the other person was responding to their treatment by the sensations I was feeling throughout my body.

I was 20 years young and was being groped by men every night. I wanted desperately for my life to be different. I hated having to look a certain way so I could swoon the men out of their money. I hated men, hated my sick mom, and I hated myself.

The deeper I went with my massage studies and energy healing the more present I became to the suffering of the soul. Not just my soul, but also the souls of the people I touched. The new goal was to transform the trauma. The desire to change my life and to heal the soul had overcome my being through her teachings.

CHAPTER 4

Medicate to Meditate

Heading to China after graduation seemed like the greatest idea EVER. There was a class of 20 students from America learning to become certified in the practice of Qigong and Meditation. Qigong is an ancient Chinese healthcare system that combines physical postures of body, breathing techniques and strong mental focus, and moving meditation.

For two weeks straight, we sat on the edge of our chairs in search of peace. Like an onion, layer-by-layer, we peeled back the mind. Our teacher, a small man born and raised in China, kept telling us to picture ourselves on the top of a mountain. I am sure that most of us wanted to jump off the "fucking mountain" at that point. I had never witnessed such weeping. There was nowhere to go and nothing to do except sit, be with the pain and contemplate. By the end of those two weeks, I threw away the bottle of Xanax I had been taking since I was 18. My new mantra was "meditate, not medicate."

Here I was, 23 years young on multiple daily doses of Xanax. It seemed like the only way to cope with my mother and her head injuries. I was annoyed and frustrated with all people. I couldn't stand the looks on their face, the tone of their voice, people made my skin crawl. I remember driving down the street seeing neighborhood garden globes and thinking, I want to smash them on the concrete.

My stress responses made me want to either strangle everyone or kill myself. I felt awful. When I went to our family doctor for help, he pressed pharmaceuticals. Never once did he question or mention proper diet or meditation.

Traditional Chinese Medicine truly healed my being. Beginning Qigong and learning to meditate saved my life. It was intense work; to sit for 5 hours a day and face one's self. Transformational to say the least; it sure beat suppressing emotions and masking who I was with Xanax.

The tour of the Beijing hospital where I was training was eye opening. There were people being treated with herbal IV's, herbs being injected into the body for rapid healing of brain, organs and the body as a whole. There were rooms of tiny drawers filled with herbs and animal parts, adult playgrounds on the premises to keep active for good lymph flow. This Chinese healthcare system is over five thousand years old. My eyes were suddenly wide-open to its whole body healing methods; Western medicine has much to learn.

Chapter 5

India

Ek Ong Kar
Sat Nam
Kartaa Purkh Nirbhao Nirvair
Akaal Moorat
Ajoonee, Saibhong, Gur Prusaad
Aad Sach, Jugaad Sach
Hai Bhee Sach, Nanak Hosee Bhee Sach
Nanak Hosee Bhee Sach

I chanted. I chanted long and hard. I chanted long and hard staring at the wall for hours. I chanted long and hard staring at the wall for hours and hours. They told me the Mul Mantra would clear my mind and change the vibration of my body. They told me that it was so powerful it could change my fate while re-writing my destiny.

After all, they knew the key; they knew the key to the truth.

Shit, what did I have to lose?

For my twenty-fifth birthday, I set out on this journey alone seeking to enrich my life, looking for the missing pieces. I was tired of working in the strip clubs back home, pissed at every man who passed by, shaved my head out of shame and thought yoga and meditation were the answer.

Chanting, Ritual, Silence.

Chota Char Dham is a Hindu Pilgrimage circuit in the Indian Himalayas. It consisted of four different sites in different corners of the country. I covered all four sites during the seven-month pilgrimage.

Nick was a great travel partner that I had met in Rishikish and asked him if he wanted to journey into the Himalayas. We didn't speak the entire drive; he was the quiet type, which is why I picked him. We would get out along the way peacefully sharing these breathtaking views together and feeling the Earth vibrating beneath our feet. Ommmmm.

Chanting, Ritual, Silence.

We met Cal and Deb in Gangatri, Cal from the U.K. and Deb from Canada. Turned out Deb was headed to Netela for the same teacher training I had signed up for at the Sivananda Ashram. They ended up heading there in a jeep. Nick and I decided to walk the 25 miles to the nearest town.

We found ourselves tucked away in a cave taking tea with a naked Baba. There are no words to describe the experience of taking tea with this sacred being in his mountain cave. These Holy men take an oath of silence as they renounce the material world. It was our fortune that he saw us as seekers of truth and chose to take us in to share his teachings.

Chanting, Ritual, Silence.

I found myself sitting in the middle of the Himalayas in a small Hindu Pilgrim Town called Gangotri, praying to God to purify my soul. I immersed myself in these sacred rituals bathing repeatedly in the Bhagirathi River and Mother Ganges. Still, I couldn't seem to get clean from the groping hands of the past. I set out on this journey alone seeking to enrich my life, looking for the missing pieces that were never gone from me in the first place, only forgotten.

C H A P T E R   6

Dear Sissy

Dear Sissy,

I never had the chance to tell you, but you saved my life. As your death rattle filled the living room, I was on my way home from trafficking my body and a part of my soul for the last time. I stopped on the dirt road in the pitch black night, got out of the car and fell to my knees praying I would never have to feel that pain and disgust ever again. I pleaded with God that I would give up that lifestyle for good. I needed to feel secure with a place to live here in the states.

You told mom to give me the house after you died and she did. It was the answer to my prayer. You saved me. To this day, the sequence of events blows my mind. I told God I would never step foot working in those bars again. I kept my word.

I'll never forget you saying "Come and see me when you can." It's what grandma says all the time now. I can still sense the smell and the sight of cancer eating away at your right breast; the love for Uncle Sam that never died, remains with me. I will never forget mom and I standing there as you took your last breath. I slept in your hospice bed till they came to pick it up.

Mom remodeled the entire house while I was away in China. I called it your house for nearly two years after you died. I replayed the last words you said to me over and over again till I was out of tears.

The memories . . . . the garden in the back when I was a young girl, the puzzles that Uncle Sam would do on the table in the basement. Now the yoga studio is where the puzzle table used to be. Your bowling trophies are still in the same spots you left them in the garage. The rose bushes still bloom. I am reminded of your greatness night and day. Everyone who enters my home instinctively feels the love and comfort that you and Uncle Sam began there nearly 60 years ago.

Farewell Sissy, I love you.

Thank you for saving my life.

C H A P T E R   7

Polarity Process

With every breath I take, I find myself continuously pondering how the pieces of life fit together. Not a conscious breath escapes me without this review of life's connections. I now know, through my own Healing Agenda, that healing is a choice.

We have this choice every day. Before making any choice, we need to be consciously aware of how our thought processes influence what we want. What do you really want? Intention directs our life. Intention is defined as a mental state representing a commitment to carrying out an action in the present or future. What is your intention to heal? How bad do you want to heal? How deep are you willing to go?

After years of practicing massage and integrating what I learned in Asia, I was introduced to Polarity. Polarity Therapy is a form of Energy Medicine that understands the body as consciousness and focuses on the release of tension and blocked energy in the body, brain and organs. It is a form of Somatic Psychology. Somatic Therapy is a holistic therapy that studies the relationship between the mind and body in regard to psychological past. The theory behind Somatic Therapy is that trauma systems are the effects of instability of the autonomic nervous system. Past traumas disrupt the nervous system. Polarity Therapy facilitates healing on the deepest levels and accelerates evolution of our Being.

I quit the strip clubs for good, once I moved home from India and into Sissy's home. The Polarity Center became the next step in my Healing Agenda. Over the course of six years, all Polarity Courses were completed. My life was changed. The trauma of growing up without my father, the deep self-hate and soul abuse had finally come to an end. Through freeing up blockages of energy and stress in and out of the body, a miracle alignment occurred. After 31 years, with my energies in a new space, my father suddenly reentered my world.

Polarity is an ongoing process of life. One must be grounded in their intention to heal. Pain and suffering, choices of change, the process of healing; it's all energy. We are all energy beings. There is nothing but energy.

P.S. It's all an illusion.

CHAPTER 8

Father

The date is 1/4/14 and I'm standing with my mother on one side and father on the other, staring at father's identical twin lying in a casket. It was like looking into a mirror. The duality of seeing father's image in a casket, after all, he had been dead to me for years. Back in my body, I see father is crying as he turns to my mother and I. He embraces us. I have often wondered what it would be like to feel the presence of my parents holding me in a triangle of love. I sensed the electrical surge straight down to my soul. The presence of both their arms wrapped around my body felt magical and right.

Father turned to a woman and man next to him and introduced me as their niece. Mind you, both of whom I am meeting for the first time and never knew I was born. It's hard to describe what it feels like to meet "family" that never knew you existed. Did I mention I am thirty-one?

As the day went on, father kept introducing me to everyone that entered the funeral home. My mom kept busy speaking with old friends as she watched him introduce me as his daughter. Which he never claimed till now. Just when I thought the situation couldn't get more bizarre, my mother walks up to father and a group of his friends and says, "aren't you going to introduce your old lay?" Talk about some old demons being released. Can you say mortified?

My mother and father never married. Father was never present in his own life, so how could he be present in his child's?

Every one of father's friends that I met, stared me up and down then dropped their jaw. I mean come on, what a grand slam funeral! You come to mourn for a man who died in a car accident.

The next thing you know, old family secrets are revealed from thirty-one years ago. Surprise!

The following months after the funeral were surreal. There was a new closeness with father while I barely spoke with my mom. I was aware of the foundational healing happening at the very core of all of our beings. The search to find the truth of my existence had come to an end. Dad threw me a birthday party in October; there was a cake with my name and a big 32 on it. He wrote me a song that he sang to me about becoming a family, after all these years.

Mind you never one birthday card, not one penny of child support throughout my life, and then this beautiful cake and party.

Really?

CHAPTER 9

The Medicine

Sustaining the relationship with my father was easy and natural throughout the year following his twin's death. I look back now and recognize that it was due to serving as the role of healer and not his daughter. I thought I had healed completely. I thought that life had brought about this miraculous healing of forgiveness. I was 32 years young and finally thought I had a father for good.

I recognized my humanness still held onto anger despite my higher self's understanding. The work with the Medicine changed those thoughts and brought about a whole new experience. This master plant, Ayahuasca, is ingested through a tea in the Amazonian Rainforest in a ceremony with Indigenous Healers. You drink the tea and sit in silence. The Shamans begin their healing songs known as Icaros to invoke the spirit of the vine. The journey among dimensions begins. I believe this experience is the deepest healing known to man.

Shortly after working with the Medicine locally, I flew to Iquitos, Peru to a spiritual center to study with a group of Shamans. The ceremonies were large consisting of people from Croatia, France, Netherlands, Toronto, and United States. Four nights a week we sat in ceremony delving deeper into ourselves on psychological and spiritual levels similar to psychotherapy sessions.

We listened to the Icaros and the rave of the jungle around the Maloka. Maloka is an indigenous word for house. Each 5-hour ceremony is equivalent to 10 years of psychotherapy. By the end of my visit, I had lost 11 pounds of emotional baggage; stirring up heavy emotions surrounding situations in which I thought were resolved.

I realize that our lessons evolve. We will always have new lessons while we are on this journey called life. The fact is, when it comes to healing it may take lifetimes. We merely enter deeper states in our Being where we can accept them differently as we gradually rise in consciousness.

It is our responsibility as spiritual beings in human form to continuously work towards transformation of the soul. Simply being born, leads to a lifelong journey; that we as individuals experience as our own Healing Agenda.

Aho
Gracias

Printed in the United States
By Bookmasters